FOLENS

IDEAS BANK

ANCIENT GREECE

Sally Elding
Rachel Prior

Contents

Folens
Publishers

How to use this book

Ideas Bank books provide you with ready to use, practical photocopiable activity pages for your children **plus** a wealth of ideas for extension and development.

TEACHER IDEAS PAGE   PHOTOCOPIABLE ACTIVITY PAGE

Clear focus to the activity.

Suggestions for developing work on the photocopiable pages.

Background information and other help given.

Extension activities suggested to take the work one step further.

Independent activities for children to work with.

● Time saving, relevant and practical, **Ideas Bank** books ensure that you will always have work ready at hand.

Cover by: In Touch Creative Designs Ltd.   Illustrations by: Philip Hodgson.   Cover photo © Trustees of British Museum.

First published 1993 by Folens Limited, Albert House, Apex Business Centre, Boscombe Road, Dunstable, LU5 4RL, England.

ISBN 185276513-5   Printed in Singapore by Craft Print

GREEK WHO'S WHO

Name	Function	Family	Symbols
APHRODITE	Goddess of love and beauty	Daughter of Uranus. Mother of Eros, Aeneas and Harmonia	Roses, doves and sparrows
APOLLO	God of sun, light and music	Son of Zeus and Leto. Brother of Artemis	Laurel tree or Laurel wreath
ARES	God of war	Son of Zeus and Hera. Twin brother of Eris. Father of Eros and Harmonia	Spear and helmet
ARTEMIS	Goddess of the moon, hunting and wild animals	Daughter of Zeus and Leto. Sister of Apollo	Cypress tree, deer, dogs
ATHENA	Goddess of wisdom and war	Daughter of Zeus and Metis.	An owl and an olive tree.
DEMETER	Goddess of crops and farming	Daughter of Cronos and Rhea. Mother of Persephone. Sister of Zeus and Poseidon	Wheat and barley
DIONYSUS	God of wine and the theatre.	Son of Zeus and Semele. Husband of Ariadne. Had six sons.	The Thrysos - a stick entwined with leaves from a vine.
HEPHAESTUS	God of fire and industry	Son of Zeus and Hera. Brother to Hebe, Ares and Eris	The hammer and the anvil.
HERA	Goddess of marriage and children	Daughter of Cronos and Rhea. Wife of Zeus. Mother of Ares, Hephaestus, Eris and Hebe	The peacock.
HERMES	Messenger of the gods	Son of Zeus and Maia	Winged sandals and helmet.
HESTIA	Goddess of the home	Daughter of Cronos and Rhea	The hearth and eternal fire
POSEIDON	God of the sea and earthquakes	Son of Cronos and Rhea. Brother of Zeus. Married Amphitrite. Father of Polyphemus	A trident
ZEUS	King of the gods. God of the sky or heavens	Son of Cronos and Rhea. Brother of Posiedon, Hera, Demeter and Hestia	A thunder bolt, an eagle and an oak tree

The land of Ancient Greece -

Aims

The aim of this activity is to introduce knowledge and understanding of the area in which most of Ancient Greek History is placed, using map locations and research skills to discover the most important cities.

Background

The land of Ancient Greece was centred upon the mainland and islands that we know as Greece today. But it was much wider, as it included coastal places bordering the Mediterranean that the Greeks influenced through battles, trade links and farming.

Activity

- Use world maps of Europe to locate the area of study. Relate it to the child's locality in terms of distance and direction.
- Draw on the experiences of children and other adults who have been to the area on holiday.
- On the base map are marked eight cities of Ancient Greece. What are they? (Teacher may provide the answers after pupils have been involved in map searching).
- Is there anything associated with the place, e.g. a building, person or event.
- Research into these buildings, peoples and events and write a Guide Book to the Ancient Cities of Greece. Why do we still remember them today?
- Compare with a map of the area today - do these ancient cities still exist?

Developments

- Add other places on to the base map as they are investigated through the topic such as places mentioned in stories, battles, names of seas, islands, etc. Collect picures of Greek sites from travel brochures or postcards and link with string to the locality on the map.
- Place a grid square over the map and give the locations of each city. Use simple number co-ordinates and children can invent their own symbols for the squares, e.g. a helmet, an owl.
- Use the base map for physical geography information about Greece, e.g. names of mountains and rivers.
- Each city had its own coin symbol. Athens adopted an owl as its symbol as it was one of the symbols of Athena after whom the city was named. Look at pictures of Greek coins and design a coin for each of the cities on the map. You could use appropriate letters from the Greek alphabet (see page 36) to label or decorate them.
- Compare to original Greek coins.

Answers

1. **Athens** - most important city containing the Acropolis
2. **Sparta** - famous for its tough soldiers
3. **Marathon** - famous for its battle
4. **Delphi** - famous for its temple and oracle
5. **Olympia** - home of the Olympic Games
6. **Argos** - home of Danae (visited by Zeus as a shower of gold), daughter of Acrisius, the King. King Eurystheus gave Heracles his twelve labours.
7. **Mycenae** - the palace of Agamemnon
8. **Troy** - famous for its besieged city and the Trojan Wars

The land of Ancient Greece

Use this map to label the important towns and cities numbered and any other features which are important - rivers, seas, mountain ranges, islands, etc.

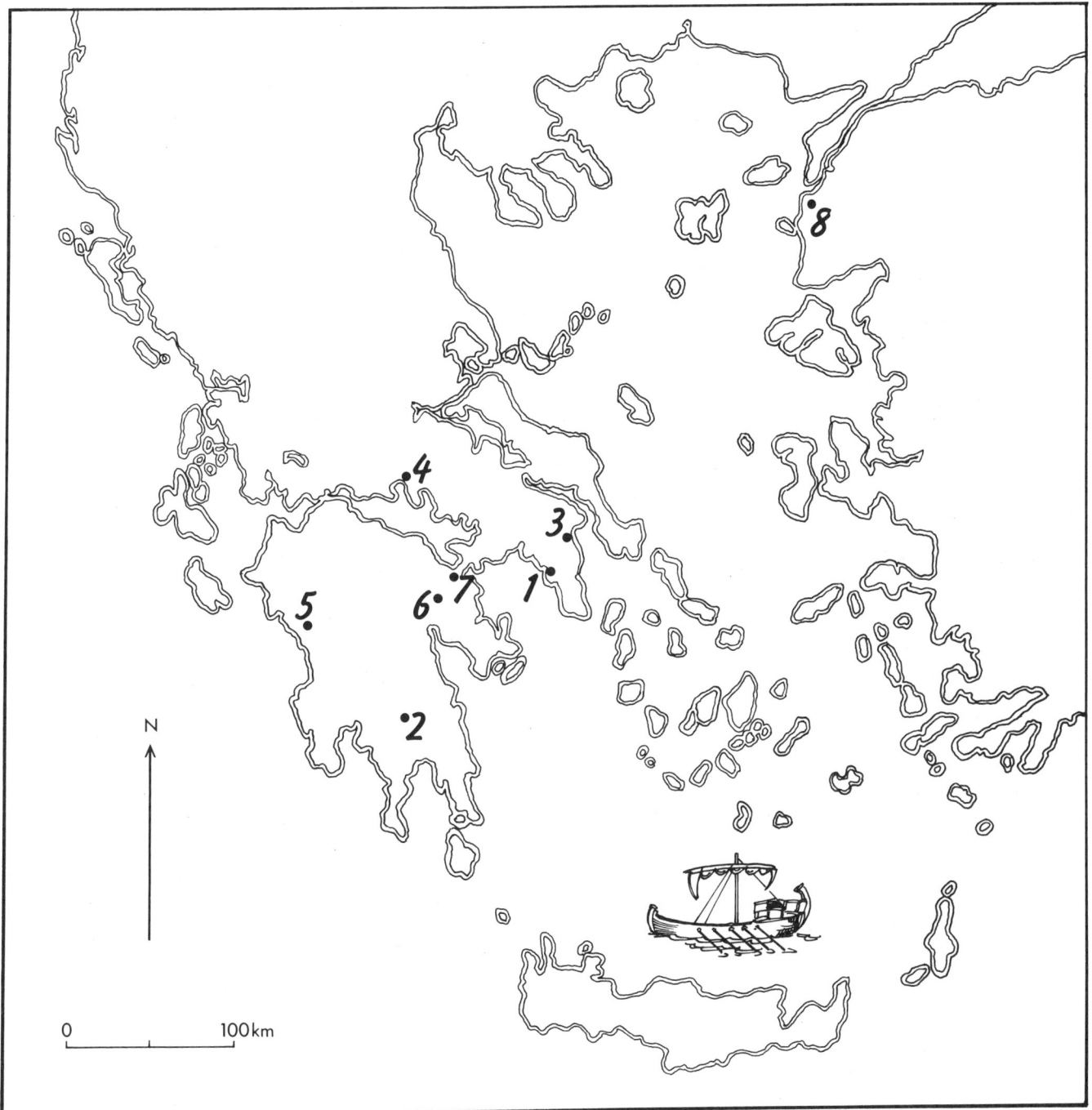

N

0   100km

1. _____

2. _____

3. _____

4. _____

5. _____

6. _____

7. _____

8. _____

    This page may be photocopied for classroom use only   5

The Gods - Ideas Page

Aims

The aim here is to introduce to the pupils the Greek gods. The pupils will have to draw upon their research skills and then will take on the role of their investigated character to interpret motives and the consequences of their actions.

Activity

- Read the class/group a Greek myth which involves the gods in action and discuss the actions and the motivation of the god/s. Discuss the possible character of the god/s.
- Discuss the passport in front of them.
Look at and discuss the kind of information needed and the writing of the character, e.g. Zeus - what would he want to be called? Just 'a god' or 'King of the Gods'?
Where would he live?
Information can be gathered about Mount Olympus. What kind of features would the god/goddess have? Do these change? Perhaps read a story where the god transposes himself into another form - Zeus/Danae and the shower of gold.

HELIOS

- Allocate each child a god or goddess - see page 3.
- Each child uses books to find out about whichever god/goddess is under discussion.
- Each child records the information on the passport.

Developments

- Each child thinks about the adventures of the god/goddess: 'Think about the adventures in your life and the famous things you have done. Select the best episode and write MY STORY'.
- The group come together and read their stories. Do the character studies match up with the other people's ideas of the mythological characters. If not, why not?
- Children play their characters in role. They sit in front of a group and answer questions in role - 'I am ...', 'I look like ...'
- Characters should give reasons for their actions, e.g. 'I went to war with Troy because ...'
- Place stories in sequence paying attention to the consequences of the characters' actions.
- Discuss whether myths and legends are reliable as historical sources, e.g. about wars. If not, why not?
- Find out who the gods/goddesses are related to: 'My name is ... My brother is ... My cousin is ...' This is important in Greek mythology as the characters in many of the stories are interrelated.
- Begin to compile family trees for display.

Extra Ideas

- Design a cover for the passport. What might it have on the front to make it particularly special to that god? Many gods/goddesses had their own symbols, e.g. Trident of Neptune.
- Make solid covers for the passports in shapes, e.g. Greek pillars - some research will be necessary to distinguish between the various sorts, Greek patterns - various amphorae can be studied and the patterns copied and incorporated into design work.

DIONYSUS
ARES
NEPTUNE

The Gods

My Story

Name

Address

Physical Features

Any other information

Aims

Here, the text and pictures to a very simple story are used. They follow a familiar pattern; a setting with a main character; a number of episodes with a problem and resolution leading towards a final conclusion. An awareness of story grows through involvment with stories. This activity offers one approach which could be used with other simple story lines to gain a better awareness of historical narrative and historical sources. You can consider any Greek god in this way.

Background

The chosen character here is Athena, daughter of Zeus and goddess of wisdom and war. The story of the birth of Athena can be found in most good reference books and is a good visual story.
- Tell or read the story to the pupils. Legend says she sprang fully armed from the head of Zeus and she fought with Poseidon for the rule of Attica. Poseidon produced the horse, but Athena produced the olive. This was considered more useful and so Athens was named after her. She was worshipped on the Acropolis and the Parthenon was built in her honour (parthenos = virgin) to contain a huge gold statue of her.

Activity

The teacher can either give the text or the pictures to the pupils to sequence.
- Pupils with pictures could be asked to write their own text to match.
- Pupils with the text could be asked to draw their own pictures to match.

Developments

- Look at other stories associated with Athena:
  - The reason why crows are black.
  - The weaving challenge with Arachne.
  - The naming of Athens.
- Develop your own fables in the style of Aesop. Set them in Ancient Greek times, using Greek characters. Why are magpies black and white? Why do snakes not walk? Dramatise these stories.
- Research the symbols of Athens, e.g. the olive tree and the owl. It is easy to produce a card game from this information. See page 3 for useful information to make three sets of cards: the god, the symbol, the function of the god. Children have to match up all three correctly.
- Design the cards and even the box to put them in. Use traditional Greek designs and patterns. Make this a larger project by getting the children to write the rules and print them using the word processor. Writing rules that everybody can understand is not an easy option!
- Athens was the cultural capital of Ancient Greece. What famous buildings can children name? Use modern travel brochures and guide books to see what remains of the ancient splendour. Look closely at the Acropolis - what might it have looked like when it was complete? Make simple models to show its structure.

The Birth of Athena

Zeus was walking beside lake Triton	
He began to get a headache	
He ordered Hepaestus, his son to crack his skull	
A lump formed where Zeus had been hit	
It grew bigger and bigger	
Finally, out of the lump came his daughter Athena wearing full armour	

This page may be photocopied for classroom use only

Aims

The texts of two lesser-known myths are introduced. They pose a question for pupils to discuss before transposing the story into a play for others to listen to and watch. Children should be introduced to the problems of using story or myth as historical source material and the dangers in interpretation.

Background

What is a myth? Chambers Dictionary defines a myth as, '... an ancient traditional story of gods or heroes, especially offering an explanation of some fact or phenomenon: a story with a veiled meaning.'
- Discuss with children if myths are useful historical sources. If not, why not?
- Myths are generally used to explain a difficult phenomenon.

Activity

- Share the stories with the pupils. Allow enough time for the questions to be discussed.
- If pupils are not familiar with play-writing it would be an ideal opportunity to look at this genre now. In particular, point out features such as layout, scene details, stage directions, instructions for the actors on expression and tone of voice, sound effects, etc.
- Pupils could take either story and write as a play.

Developments

- Performances of the plays could take a variety of forms:
  - pupils acting it out themselves.
  - perform it as a radio play.
  - using stick or shadow puppets on a model stage made by the pupils.
- Make Greek costume, e.g. What is the difference between a Peplos and a Chiton? How are they fastened? Why was dress so simple? Would it have anything to do with the fact that they could only weave small rectangular shapes? Why did fashion not change so quickly as it does today?
- The naming of places could be taken further. Are there reasons for the names of other Greek cities? If not, can pupils create their own reasons and stories.
- Try to discover other pairings in Greek legends - Orpheus and Eurydice, Echo and Narcissus, Persephone and Pluto. The children should research the story surrounding chosen characters and be able to retell from one of the characters point of view.
- Investigate all the myths related to one god or take an explanation of an event, e.g. the creation of the world, and find parallels in other cultures - Egyptian, Chinese, Aztec.

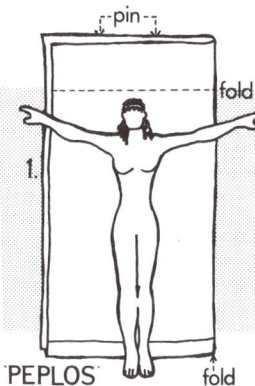

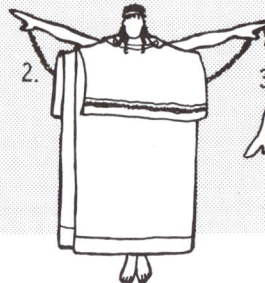

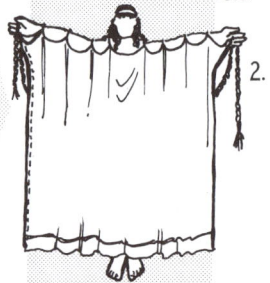

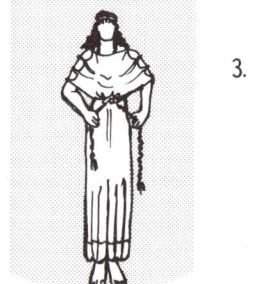

Myths

THE ALMOND TREE

Phyllis and Acamas were very much in love. Acamas had to go away to fight in the Trojan Wars. He was away fighting for many years. Phyllis was sad because she missed him terribly and was on the point of entering the Underworld when Athena took pity on her and transformed her into an Almond tree.

Acamas returned from the war and when he discovered that Phyllis was changed, he was overcome with grief. He searched for the Almond tree. Unlike all the other trees around it, it had no leaves upon its branches. On finding it he wrapped his arms around it and kissed it. As he did so, the Almond tree burst with blossom.

WHAT WAS SO UNUSUAL ABOUT THE ALMOND TREE BURSTING WITH BLOSSOM?

THE NAMING OF A CITY

Athena, goddess of wisdom and war and Poseidon the god of the sea and earthquakes argued about who should give their name to the greatest city in Greece. They decided that whichever of them gave the town the greatest gift would have the city named after them.

Poseidon went first - he struck his trident into the rock on which the city was built ... out of this place poured a stream of water which flowed to the sea and gave its citizens their first route for ships so that it could make trade routes and so become wealthy and powerful.

Athena decided to give the town one of her own creations - an olive tree. This would give food and precious oil to the citizens to use and export.

WHICH WAS THE GREATEST GIFT? WHY?
WHO THEN WAS THE CITY NAMED AFTER - POSEIDON OR ATHENA?

Aims

Using the Greek myth Theseus and the Minotaur, this activity will involve the pupils in learning more about the importance of myth and legend to Greek history as well as using directional skills and the language required for this.

Background

The minotaur was a monstrous creature, half-man and half-bull, child of Minos, the King of Crete. It was kept in a maze of passages and young men and women were sacrificed to it. Theseus was the national hero of Athens and volunteered to be a part of this sacrifice. Adriadne, Minos' daughter loved Theseus and enabled him to escape the maze by giving him string to mark his path. He killed the monster and they escaped together.

- Tell the story of Theseus and the Minotaur. You may wish to discuss the story and look at or talk about mazes, particularly ones the children have visited.
- In relation to this, talk about how easy it is to loose your sense of direction - why/how does this happen. Who has a good/ bad sense of direction?

CRETE
Knossos
Gournia
Phaestos

Activity

- Each pupil marks on to the maze the route taken by Theseus.
- Underneath, the route taken should be recorded. This could be done in one of two ways:
  - either in terms of left, right, forwards or backwards.
  - Or in terms of north, south, east, west.

Developments

- Using the same maze, a 3D model could be constructed from Lego or, on the floor with Duplo, the Turtle or Roamer could then be used. New mazes can be created using the floor maze for other pupils to solve.
- Create mazes using the computer. This is good practise in measuring and in manipulation of the keyboard and mouse.
- What other creatures could Theseus meet within the maze? Draw and describe these. Make them in clay and place these somewhere on the route. A board game could be developed from this.

- The Minotaur was a fearsome creature, but what did he really look like? Produce a warning poster for the creature.
- What other monsters can be found in Greek myths?
  - What did they look like?
  - Where did they live?
  - Who had to confront and fight them?
  - What was the result?

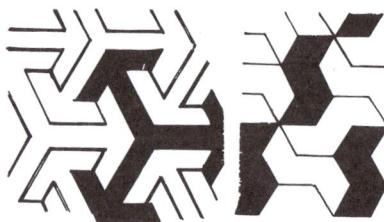

- Use mazes in maths. Use a piece of string for measuring against a scale to see how far Theseus would have to travel. Compare this with the straight-line distance. Research into Greek mathematicians and what they contributed to the world -Pythagoras, Euclid, etc.

- Try to get information on other mazes such as the one at Hampton Court or research into the mazes and patterns created by Martin Escher. Use similar designs to create optical illusion patterns in art.
- Dramatise the meeting of Theseus and the Minotaur.
  - What happens when they first see each other?
  - How do they move around each other?
  - Who makes the first move?

The Amazing Minotaur

Tell your partner the story of Theseus and the Minotaur.
Now direct him or her through the maze by giving simple directions only.

Directions for the route:

The Tasks of Heracles - Ideas Page

Aims

This is a collaborative activity which will require the pupils to discuss all the possible ways of solving the problems faced by Heracles and then to reach a consensus.

Activity

- The tasks of Heracles are given to the pupils (one at a time or all at once - teacher to decide).
- On their own and then in groups, pupils should talk about how they should complete or solve the task. Through discussion, each group should put forward what they consider to be the 'best' solutions to the problems.
- The pupils could appoint a spokesperson for their group who could report back to the whole class. Alternatively, a scribe could be appointed who would keep a note on the final decision taken for each task.
- Groups could be asked to find a way of presenting the information to the whole class.
- End this activity by reading or telling the story of the twelve tasks of Heracles to the class so that the pupils see how Heracles solved the problems himself.

Background

Any good book on Greek myths will provide you with information on the birth of Heracles and the circumstances leading to King Eurystheus challenging him to solve the twelve seemingly impossible tasks. Tell the children this first part of the story only.

The son of Zeus and Alcmene, his famous exploits all derive from his amazing strength and courage. Heracles killed the children of King Eurystheus of Argos in a fit of madness sent by the goddess Hera. To make up for this awful act he agreed to undertake the Twelve Labours.

Developments

- Create a series of pictures for each task or transfer the scenes on to clay. You could create a frieze something like the Elgin Marbles.
- Make a commentary for a task (written/taped) and then dramatise the episode for radio, relying on sound effects only. How will the effects be made?
- Draw an illustrated map of Heracles' journey for the class wall. Groups can contribute by researching where the places were in the Ancient World, drawing and writing accounts to be pasted on.
- Task 13 - What else could Heracles have been asked to do?
- Look at other stories related to challenges - ancient and modern and link into citizenship or religious education lessons.

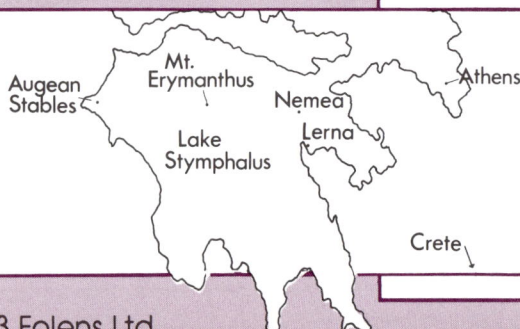

The Tasks of Heracles

How would you complete or solve the twelve tasks that faced Heracles?

YOU HAVE TO KILL THE NEMEAN LION
The lions skin is so strong no weapon will damage it.

YOU MUST DESTROY THE LEARNEAN HYDRA
The Hydra has a dog-like body with nine serpent heads. When a head is cut off, it grows back again.

CAPTURE THE CERYNEAN DEER ALIVE
This deer has hooves of bronze and horns of gold. It is swift and difficult to capture.

TRAP THE ERYMANTHIAN BOAR
This is a very large, fierce creature.

YOU HAVE TO CLEAN THE AUGEAN STABLES IN ONE DAY
The kings stables have not been cleaned for years. You may need some help.

GET RID OF THE STYMPHALIAN BIRDS
These man-eating birds have bronze beaks, claws and wings.

CAPTURE THE CRETAN BULL
This is a wild and dangerous animal.

COLLECT THE MARES OF DIOMEDES
These wild horses ate humans. Their master is Diomedes.

GET THE BELT OF QUEEN HIPPOLYTE
The belt itself will cause little problem but beware her army.

FETCH THE CATTLE OF FERYON
These cattle are guarded by Orthrus and Geryon. Orthrus is a two-headed dog. Geryon has three bodies.

YOU MUST FETCH THE GOLDEN APPLES OF HESPERIDES
You will have to ask Atlas to help you as he knows where the apples are.

FINALLY, BRING CEREBUS FROM THE UNDERWORLD
This three-headed dog guards the gates of the underworld. It can be taken but no weapons may be used.

Aims

Many of the pupils will be familiar with the story of the Trojan Horse, but this activity goes further. It gives ideas for helping pupils to understand different points of view and how deficiencies in evidence and interpretations of the past may lead to differing versions of what we know happened. A predominantly oral activity, it could lead to written work.

Preparation

You may wish to begin with no formal introduction at all. Alternatively, opportunities arise during the school day where different points of view can be highlighted - particularly playground incidents. You could note down some of these as they happen and remind the pupils of these, discussing why there are different versions of the same events.

- The children's page contains two versions of the Trojan Horse story.
  A - is the story from the Greek point of view.
  B - is the story from the Trojan point of view.
- Photocopy, cut up and place in envelopes enough copies for the children to sequence as a story.

Activity

- Divide the class into two groups - Group A and Group B and allocate an area of the classroom for each group to work in.
- Hand out the correct envelopes to the groups and working in pairs, the pupils should sequence the story.
- A pair from Group A joins with a pair from Group B and take turns to share their stories.
- Come together as a whole class to discuss issues arising from the activity in particular, similarities and differences between the two versions of the story and the reasons why this might be.

Backgound

Helen was married to Menelaus, brother of Agamemnon. When she fell in love with Paris (a trick of the gods) and eloped to Troy with him, Menelaus sought to get her back by calling on Agamemnon's help to attack Priam, King of Troy. So began the Trojan War which lasted, according to Homer, for ten years. Finally it was Odysseus who thought of the idea of the wooden horse. It was left outside the city gates and the Trojan people brought it in thinking it would bring them luck! Menelaus loved Helen so much he forgave her.

Developments

- Use the written text as a basis for a series of pictures which tell the story. The children are learning to produce a story board here which is useful for the analysis of the structure of any story or visual narrative.
- Cut up the story sections and paste them on to a class wall display of the Trojan Horse legend.
- From either version of the text, take each segment of the story and use it as the basis for a detailed paragraph of writing.
- Collect oral versions from the two storylines on tape.
- Write the story in the form of a diary from the point of view of either a Greek or a Trojan soldier.
- Discuss the story as an historical source. We know that there was an historical city of Troy and that it was destroyed. Can we be sure that it was destroyed in this particular way? What historical sources could tell us how the city was destroyed?
- How was such a (reputably) large object moved? Investigate the use of rollers and wheels. Which would have been the quickest way to move the horse under battle conditions? Make small models to demonstrate these principles. How could a fair test be arranged? How could children best record their results?

The Trojan Horse

A

B

A	B
Long, long ago, so the story goes, our beautiful Queen Helen of Sparta was captured and forced to live in the city of Troy by a brutal prince called Paris.	Long, long ago, so the story goes, a foreign Queen called Helen came to live in our wonderful city of Troy.
A large army of our loyal soldiers led by the brave Agamemnon set sail for Troy to save Queen Helen and bring her safely home.	An army of soldiers arrived some time later and camped outside the city walls. They wanted her to return to Greece with them.
After many years of fierce fighting, our courageous men hatched a brilliant plan. They pretended to retreat and left behind a huge, magnificent wooden horse within sight of the city gates of Troy.	Many years of fierce fighting followed. When it seemed that they had finally had enough, they left. Outside the city gates we found a huge, monstrous wooden horse.
From a safe distance, our soldiers waited and watched as the Trojan people struggled to drag the horse through the gates. They chuckled with glee.	When we were sure that they had finally left, some of our citizens wheeled the horse through the gates so that we could have a closer look.
That very night, without warning, our soldiers who all the time had been hiding inside the horse, let themselves out. They silently unlocked the city gates.	That very night, much to the surprise of our people, Greek soldiers crept out from inside the horse and opened the city gates.
Finally then, the rest of the army, waiting close by, poured through the gates and ransacked the city.	Finally, the rest of the Greek army who had stayed close by, charged through the gates and attacked us, setting fire to much of the city.

The Battle of Marathon - *Ideas Page*

Aims

Pupils will be introduced to the details of a famous battle. It was an important victory for the Greeks, remembered because of the superior military strategy of a soldier called Miltiades. The details of the battle are explored in words and pictures.

Background

It was at Marathon in 490BC that due to the genius of Miltiades, a brave band of Greek soldiers decisively defeated a much larger Persian army led by King Darius. The battle took place on a plain between the sea and the mountains.
The 192 Athenian warriors who died in the battle were buried on the spot under a mound of earth 30ft high and 600ft at the base. This mound was excavated at the end of the 19th century and the remains of men and sacrificial animals plus black figure pottery were found.

Activity

- Use the map showing the important cities of Ancient Greece to locate Athens and Marathon.
- Children research or you explain the tactics used by Miltiades in this battle.
- Look at the information sheet relaying the details of the Battle of Marathon. Sequence the events and annotate the map using this information.
- Taking the role of either a Persian or an Athenian, pupils should record their battle memories - either taped or written, including such information as:
  - what part they played in the battle.
  - what in their view went well or wrong.
  - where were they in the heat of the battle, in the Persian line-up or the Athenian phalanx.

Shields were normally round and large enough to protect the soldier's body between neck and thigh. They were made of bronze and leather.
Helmets were made of bronze. Some had horse-hair crests.

Developments

- Discuss the ways in which historians could be so sure about the details of the battle. What could their sources have been? How reliable are they?
- Draw or design and make models of the equipment used in battle, e.g. the catapult, the bellows, the battering ram and the siege towers.

catapult

siege tower

battering ram

- Make a 3D representation of the battle-field and re-enact the Battle of Marathon.
- Research the background to other battles, e.g. The Battle of Salamis and The Siege of Troy. In particular, investigate the military tactics used by the foot soldiers and the cavalry in some of these battles. Make annotated drawings illustrating the tactics used.
- Investigate the development of ships of the time and their role in war, particularly the advantages and disadvantages of the Trireme.
- A hoplite (foot soldier) was able to choose his own shield decoration. This was often associated with his family or city. Ask children to design their own shield decoration to include their own family or city symbols.

The Battle of Marathon

Put the stages of the Battle of Marathon into the correct order.
Talk about the most important facts and then put the information on the map,
so you can explain the battle to somebody else.

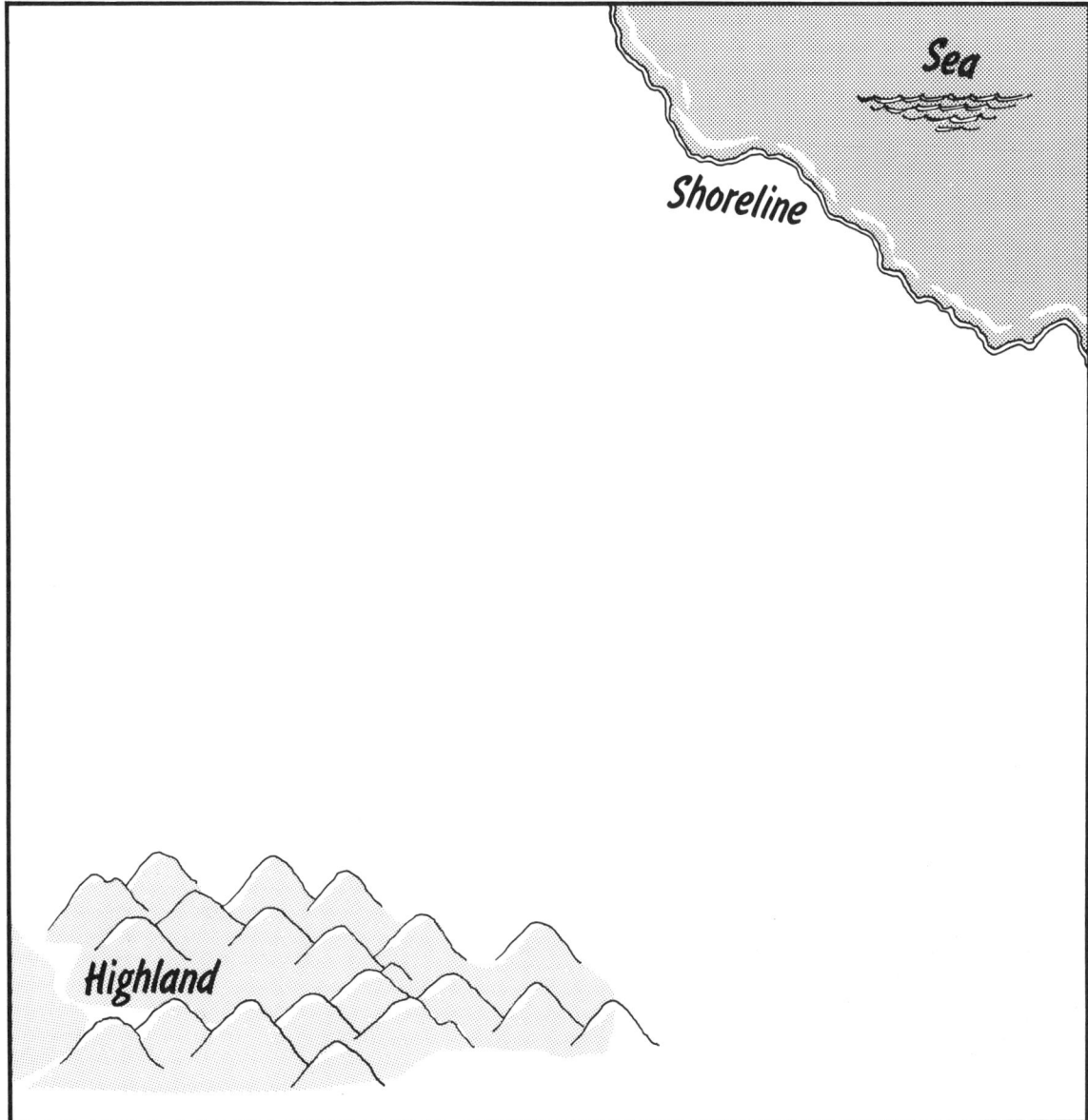

Sea

Shoreline

Highland

◆ The battle had been won.
◆ A smaller Athenian army led by Miltiades marched overland from Athens to meet them.
◆ A large Persian army, led by King Darius landed at Marathon, a coastal city north-east of Athens.
◆ A fierce battle took place on the lowland between the sea and the hills.
◆ The block of soldiers or phalanx pushed and pushed forward until the Persian army fell.
◆ Organising themselves into blocks eight soldiers deep, the Athenian army moved towards the Persians.

Aims

The Greeks held a belief as to the appearance of the world and the places reached after death. In this activity, children begin to explore these different areas.

Preparation

- Begin with a story dealing with a Greek version of the Underworld - Persephone is a good one - or introduce the terms on the photocopiable sheet.
- Each child chooses or is given a place he/she going to go in this new world. This can lead to fruitful discussion of their self-image. Where do they think they ought to go? Where might other people think they ought to go?

Activity

- Where are you going? What will it be like? Children should think about their conceptions of the various places and perhaps be made aware of stereotypes. Where have they got these images from? Children could talk about films they have seen or books they have read that concern themselves with images of these places.
- After thinking/talking about their place they should create it on paper. Use this sheet first as it gives the less able an equal chance. More able groups can develop their work into another medium later.
- After creating the scene the groups should meet up with other travellers going to the other worlds and discuss their representations of the underworld. How and why do they differ? What features are the same? Why should this be?
- Finally all the views should be combined to make one underworld image. What can this tell us about the Ancient Greeks perception of the afterlife? How is it different from ours, or from other peoples in the world today?

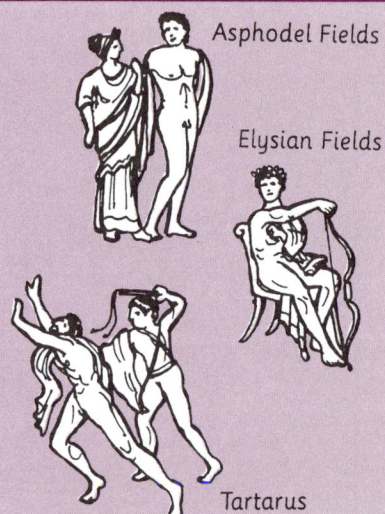

Asphodel Fields

Elysian Fields

Tartarus

Developments

- The one Underworld image can be presented as a class wall display or a 3D area which people actually travel through. This gives opportunity for groups to make props/rooms/walls/costumes/hats, etc and think about sound effects and lighting to create atmosphere which deals with many science and technology issues.

- Write a description of the Underworld. How did the children feel at various stages of their journey?
- Use other written modes - a letter back from the Underworld, a diary entry of your journey found by the next traveller.
- Creating a specific area, no matter whether imaginary or not, gives plenty of scope for mapping skills in geography and the use of specific vocabulary - location (next to), direction (which way?), perspective (2D/3D), representation (signs and symbols), scale, etc.

- Children should describe to others accurately how they move about in their and other worlds developing speaking and listening skills.
- RE ideas of the 'other world' have to be sensitively discussed, but can offer a comparison to the religious beliefs of the Greeks.
- Crossing the River Styx. Who is Charon? What is he like? What is his background? Written work and artwork can arise from this. One child might like to take on the character and sit in the 'hot seat' while the others ask for information.

Beyond the River Styx

MOUNT OLYMPUS
The home of the Greek Gods. The highest part of the Greek world.

EARTH
The place where you live. Mysterious creatures also live here and have many battles with the gods.

RIVER STYX
When you die, Charon the Ferryman takes you across to the Underworld, providing he has been paid.

Where will you go? What will it be like?

Asphodel Fields –
the place for ordinary people.

Tartarus –
the place where evil people go.

Elysian Fields –
the resting place of good heroic people.

This page may be photocopied for classroom use only

The Underworld - Ideas Page

Aims

This is a further investigation centred around the Greeks' belief of the Underworld. The children are considering the organisation of the area by creating a map and interpreting evidence.

Preparation

- Read a Greek myth which involves the underworld - e.g. Orpheus and Eurydice.
- Introduce the terms of the concepts which are printed on the photocopiable page.
- The children will need something to draw with.
- It would be best for them all to use the space on the paper at first - children can develop their work on larger sheets of paper later.

Developments

- Show the children other maps, e.g. Ordnance Survey maps and discuss the various features of them. What symbols are used on OS maps? How is the scale represented? How do you measure distance on a map? Is scale important on a map of a mythological space? Is colour important to distinguish the features on their maps?
- Groups should meet to discuss the differences between their underworld maps and talk about why the maps do not have to be the same. Is this to do with the evidence which is available from stories and myths? Is this evidence reliable? If not, why not?
- The maps could all be displayed. Borders could be designed from Greek patterns.
- In pairs develop the map into a board game. What is the aim of your game? What are the rules? These will have to be as clear and concise as possible. The board and the counters would have to be designed and made. Would you have chance cards? What styles and patterns would be used? Are there any computer games which involve Greek Myths?
- Make a 3D model of the Underworld. You could use a cardboard box or a shoe box for this. What problems are there in changing a 2D plan into a 3D model? How do you create rocks? Water? How are people going to view it? Through tissue paper to give an eerie atmosphere? Will you need lighting of a special kind to create an atmosphere? Design a light using a simple circuit and a battery.
- How do you move through this world? Create a sound score using simple class-made instruments to accompany the mime. How would Charon move and behave?
- Give directions to reach the various places. This is always more difficult than people think. Children should follow instructions exactly to start with, just to show how awful people are at giving accurate directions. Make this into a game.
- Opportunities for RE are endless here. All major religions have views on what happens after someone dies. Children could find out about these views and compare them.

Activity

- The maps should be drawn in groups of two or three so the maximum of discussion is possible.
- Stress that there is not necessarily a correct answer and that all of the maps might be different.
- Children must consider carefully where they would locate the different features of the Underworld.
- What symbols would they use on the map?

The Underworld

- Create a map of the Underworld to include these places:

Asphodel Fields

Tartarus

Elysian Fields

The Isles of the Blessed

The Palace of Pluto and Persephone

The Pool of Memory

The Pool of Lethe (forgetfulness)

The Underworld

Aims

In this activity, the pupils will be involved in learning about the Ancient Greek theatre by designing and making a mask, developing a character and dramatising it.

Background

The origins of our theatre can be traced to Ancient Greece. Drama formed part of the celebration of some religious festivals. The City Dionysia was held every Spring in Athens in honour of Dionysus and was a drama competition. Three poets entered four plays each - three tragedies and a satyr play - a rude comic farce involving the actors being dressed in satyr costume.

The Greek theatre was held outside, first in the market places and then in large open-air stadiums or theatres - often circular (amphitheatres). Each city state had its own block of seats. Important people such as leading citizens or visitors had special stone seats reserved for them at the front. The play would be performed by actors on a platform called the proscenium, and the actors would be supported by a chorus who sang and danced in the circular floor area.

Actors in the Greek theatre (male only) wore painted masks made of stiffened material. The features and detail were simple so that they could be seen right at the back and expressions on the masks showed the characters sex, age and feelings which were greatly exaggerated. They had large open mouths to aid amplification.

Activity

- Children should be made aware of characteristics of Greek theatre. Discuss the differences between children's idea of theatres and their purpose today and why theatre was so important to the Greeks.
- A design for a half-face mask has been provided. Use it to design a mask based on a tragic or a comic figure - use the role cards to help. Transfer the design on to card/papier mâché mould (or similar) and make.
- Refer back to the role cards and in pairs, plan a conversation you will have when wearing your mask.

Developments

- Make the mask 3D by using paper sculpture techniques - rolled paper for hair, folds for the nose, etc.
- Record the conversations on tape. Try different pairings. Create sound effects for the play.
- Use the tape recording to transcribe the conversations and present as a dialogue.
- Make a display of the masks, dialogues and tape recordings.
- Design and make a theatre programme advertising your own performance.
  - What shape will it be?
  - What type face could be used?
  - What decoration will there be on it?
  - Will there be any advertising inside for other Greek products or businesses?
- Photograph the masks in use. Make an album and display these.
- The images on masks needed to be seen at the back of very large theatres. Investigate which are the best combination of colours to be seen at a distance. What tests can be devised? How do you know the testing is fair? How can the children best record their results?
- Masks were also useful for amplifying sound in large areas. Test out various shapes and sizes of mouthpiece for producing the best sound over a distance. Again negotiate the problems of fair testing and recording of results.

The Theatre

Choose one of the role-play cards and then design the mask that your character would wear in the theatre.

You are Penelope, the wife of Odysseus. You have been waiting for 19 years for his return from the Trojan War. Is he dead or alive?

You are Ariadne. You have fallen in love with Theseus and have planned to help him escape from the Minotaur's maze. Now you are waiting to see if the plan has worked ...

You are Persephone. You have been kidnapped by Pluto in his chariot and taken to the Underworld. You are miserable, have not eaten but Pluto is tempting you with pomegranate seeds ...

You are King Aegeus of Athens. You long for a son to succeed you. This makes you sad. But all is not hopeless - you consult with the oracle at Delphi ...

You are Theseus, 18 years old and strong. You have never seen your father. Your mother has taken you to a secret place and told you to move a huge rock ...

You are Perseus. King Polydectes has sent you on a great adventure to find the terrifying Gorgon, Medusa and cut off her head. You are not aware of what lies ahead ...

This page may be photocopied for classroom use only

Aims

The word dialogue originates from the Greek word dialogos meaning a conversation. This activity asks children to put themselves into the role of an Ancient Greek character and talk about everyday life.

Preparation

- Talk with the children about the art of conversation.
  - What conversations do they remember?
  - What conversations have they taken part in recently?
  Compare conversation or dialogue with a monologue so that the difference is clear.
- Discuss Ancient Greek alternatives for what we know today, e.g. market = stoa.

Activity

- Act out some everyday conversations:
  - in the street
  - in the supermarket
  - in the playground.
- In pairs, use the dialogue provided and act it out. Finish writing it in your own way.
- Research everyday events in Ancient Greece that someone might talk about.
- On the right-hand side of the page rewrite the conversation, this time setting it in Ancient Greece.
- Join pairs together in order to listen to each others conversations.
- Discuss the results:
  - Have people used historical sources correctly?
  - Have people distinguished between fact and point of view?

Developments

- Tape record the conversation. Does it sound realistic? What can be done to make it sound more real? Tone of voice? Realistic detail?
- Use the dialogue as a script for drama activities. Act out and freeze frame an action. Photograph the freeze frame. Mount these photographs and make a 'true life' story as found in many comics.
- Write speech bubbles for the characters in the shots. This should be useful in enabling children to notice differences between kinds of direct speech and necessary punctuation.

- Make a collection of words changed in the Greek conversation.
- Create a dictionary of such words. Have their meanings changed very much? Can you identify any words or parts of words from Ancient Greek which are the same today?
- Produce the dialogues in the form of a comic strip. This can be done on a large scale and useful information about Ancient Greece can be incorporated, e.g. architecture, clothing, weapons and armour.
- Collect snatches of overheard conversations: '... then he fell flat on the floor ...' and create stories around them.

- Discuss the many different ways there are of beginning a conversation with someone. Make a collection of opening lines used by the children themselves, by their parents and grandparents. Has this an historical focus? How has language and convention changed? This could lead to a discussion and collection about how people in other parts of the world greet each other, e.g. the embrace of the French. This can develop a geographical focus.

Dialogos

TODAY
Outside the market place

1. Good morning.

2. Hello there, are you well?

1. Fine thank you. What about you?

2. Not too bad.
   Are you going into the market?

1. Yes I've a few things to buy for this
   evenings meal.
   I see you've already been.

2. Yes I went before the rush.
   I needed to get back for Anne
   returning from school.
   Are you having a special meal
   tonight?

1.

2.

1.

2.

1.

2.

ANCIENT GREECE
In front of the stoa

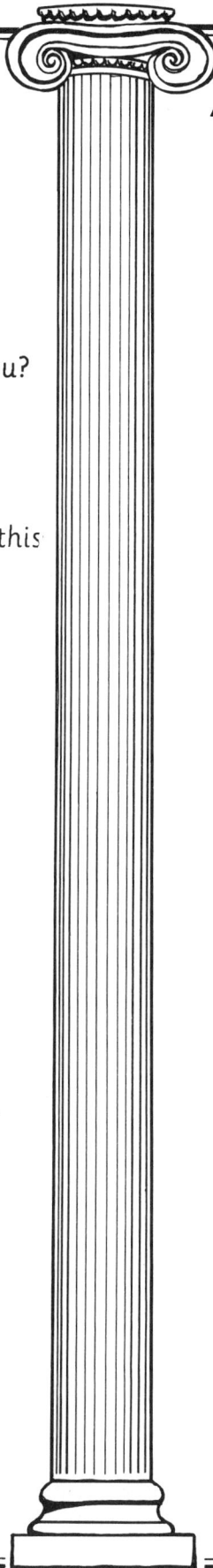

This page may be photocopied for classroom use only

Aims

An introduction to the way in which the market place operated, the role of the money changer and the range of products to be found at a typical market.

Background

The centre of every Greek city was the agora - or market place. Every city developed its own issue of coins and anyone wishing to trade with another city had to change their coins with the money changer or trapezitai who would sit at a table in the market place.

Preparation

- Copy and cut out the pupils sheet. Each group will require one produce list, so duplicate if necessary.
  Tell the children to make as much produce in the time allowed. This at the simplest level could be drawings on card:

- Produce should indicate a quantity and selling price, for example:
  cheap   =   1 to 3 coins
  average   =   4 to 6 coins
  expensive =   7 to 9 coins
  This could be determined by how long it takes to 'make' something.
- Inform each group that they must next find or make 30 coins - these could be marbles counters, etc. but each groups coins must differ.
- Groups should set up stall ready for the activity to begin. Teacher or adult will act as money changer and must also organise a common coinage.

Developments

- Design recipes for Ancient Greek dishes using these ingredients. Make (real) the food.
- There is plenty of scope for research following this activity.
  - The Agora or market
  - Introduction of coinage
  - The layout of the Agora
  - Words, e.g. stoa, metronomi, agoranomi, sitophylakes.
- The activity could be repeated after research has informed you of changes or additions. Children could write their own shopping lists.

Activity

- Explain your role as money-changer, i.e. goods can only be bought with the common coinage, so it must first be changed at the money stall. You decide on the exchange rate.
- Give out shopping lists and remind pupils that no stall should be left unattended, that rules of courtesy should be followed and they should act as real stall holders.
  Your role as money changer will be a model for this.
  The objectives are to sell the produce they have 'grown', and to buy the items on their list. Extra produce can be purchased.

Shopping

PRODUCE LIST

Leg of lamb
Pieces of pork
Hare
Wild pigeon
Chicken

PRODUCE LIST

Cabbage
Carrots
Broccoli
Tomatoes
Onions

PRODUCE LIST

Lemons
Cherries
Oranges
Melons
Grapes

PRODUCE LIST

Octopus
Prawns
Swordfish
Crab
Squid

PRODUCE LIST

Nuts (handfuls of)
Rice (bags of)
Wheat (bags of)
Barley (bags of)
Bread

PRODUCE LIST

Pieces of cheese
Pots of honey
Jugs of goat's milk
Eggs
Olives (handfuls of)

SHOPPING LIST

Leg of lamb
1 pigeon
broccoli
onion
melon
grapes
nuts
bread
cheese
goat's milk

SHOPPING LIST

3 small hares
6 tomatoes
broccoli
cherries
a melon
goat's milk
2 crabs
wheat
barley

SHOPPING LIST

2 pigeons
1 cabbage
honey
10 eggs
carrots
grapes
3 lemons
octopus pieces
barley

SHOPPING LIST

pork pieces
carrots
onions
2 lemons
2 oranges
squid
rice
honey
cheese
olives

SHOPPING LIST

1 chicken
1 small hare
broccoli
lemons
cherries
prawns
1 crab
loaf
eggs
olives

SHOPPING LIST

2 small chicken
swordfish steaks
3 large onions
4 oranges
cherries
barley
rice
olives
honey

Aims

Using geographical skills, pupils will journey around a typical Ancient Greek market place - or Agora, learning about what was sold and bought and therefore how Ancient Greeks lived from day to day.

Activity

- Each pupil needs a plan of the market. Allow time for them to study the layout and the goods available.
- Each pupil must then write a list of six different items that can be bought from the market.
- Lists are exchanged.
- On to the plan, the pupil marks the route taken to purchase the listed items, starting and finishing at the money changer.
- Lists can be exchanged as many times as you like and each shopping list recorded in a different colour.
- A more advanced version of this would be to record the route taken in directional terms.

Background

The agora was the focal point of every Greek city. It was not only used to trade but was also a meeting place and religious centre where statues of local deities would stand - often an altar too.
The basic features of a market are given. Pupils compose their own shopping lists and devise routes around the market.

Developments

- How do historians know what kinds of food were eaten or bought in Ancient Greece? What kinds of sources would be the most reliable?
- A larger plan of the agora could be created and shopping routes explored using a computer program. Scale and distances can be included and this work used for maths calculations.
- You are the owner of a market stall:
  - What is your stall?
  - What range of goods do you have?
  - Where do you get your goods from?
  - What difficulties might you have getting your goods?
  - Make up a market 'cry' to advertise your wares.
  - Design a poster to advertise your stall and its goods. What sort of language is most persuasive?
- Compare the layout of the agora with your nearest market. Draw a similar plan in order to help do this. Develop a group or class colour coding system for recording the different stalls. Use this in recording other markets visited. How do they compare in terms of layout and range of goods?

- Not all the goods at the agora were from Greece. Items came from places around the Mediterranean.
  - Where?
  - Which goods?
  - Investigate trade links between Greece and these places - i.e. how easy was it to transport goods overland or over the sea? How did political relations with countries affect these routes?
- Make lists of produce in your supermarket.
  - Find pictures of them.
  - Look at cans and packets to see where they are from.
  - How were the goods transported to your country or to the supermarket itself?
  - Produce maps to show where goods sold in markets came from.

- Each city state had its own currency system, e.g. Sparta used iron rods of different value whilst Athens had a coinage currency:
  - 6 obols = 1 drachma
  - 100 drachma = 1 mina
  - 60 minas = 1 talent.
  Use this system to make up money solving problems.
- Compare this with other currencies today. Work out exchange rates and display as charts and graphs.

The Agora

Mu   T   J   Pe   J

Fu

L

Fu

F	
Gr	V
M	P
	G
H	Fr

W	Cl
R	
C	F
Fr	V
N	

◇ M.C.

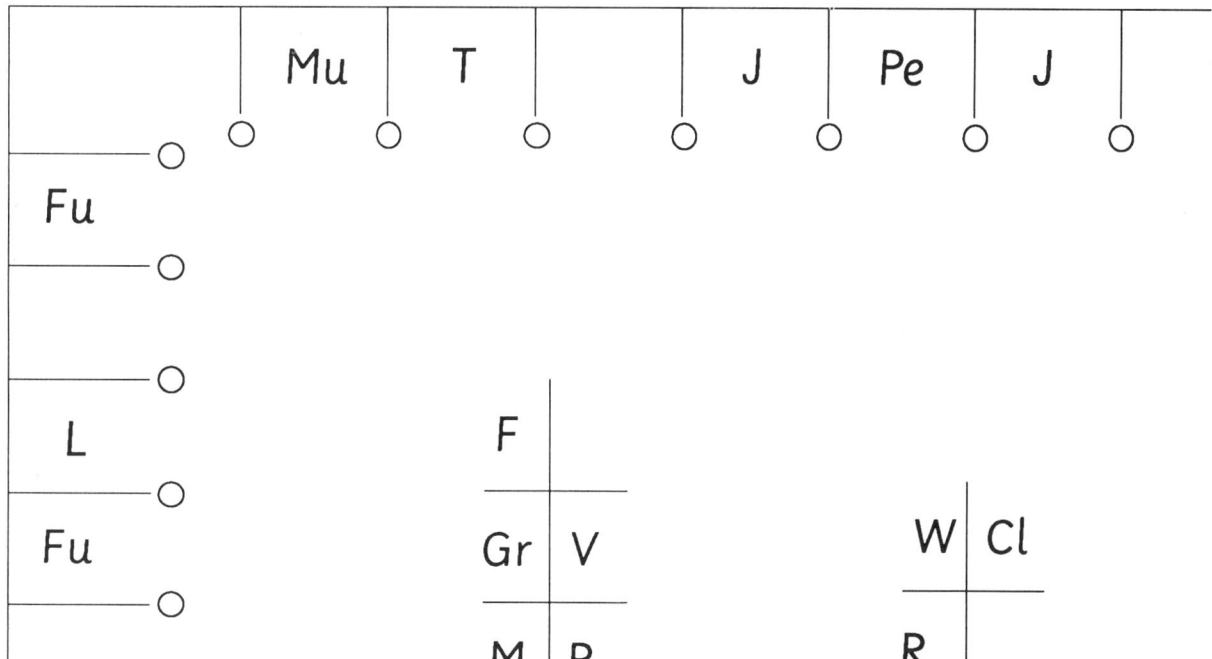

Black Smith		Weaver	Potter

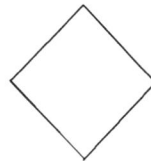

Stoa
(Covered shop area/luxury goods)

Stalls

Fu: Furniture	F: Fish	N: Nuts
Mu: Musical instruments	V: Vegetables	Gr: Grain
L: Lamps	Fr: Fruit	W: Wool
T: Toys	M: Meat	C: Chicken
J: Jewellery	G: Goat's milk	Cl: Cloth
Pe: Perfume, oils	H: Honey	R: Rugs
M.C. Money Changer	P: Pottery	

Aims

Here, pupils are introduced to some of the more interesting aspects of the Greek way of governing and of their legal system. This demands that they comment on historical sources given and look at historical change.

Activity

Diagrams of objects used in the legal system of Ancient Greece are shown on the pupils page.

- Working in groups or individually, pupils should research the objects.
- Replicas and working models should be made and used to explain to others how they worked or why they were used.

Background

Government in Sparta consisted of **a monarchy** - 2 royal families with minimal powers, basically led their people to war; **overseers of the state** - 5 men elected annually; **a council** made up of the 2 kings and 28 men over 60 - made laws, acted as judges; **an assembly** - 30 citizens over 30 - supported or rejected proposals of council. NB. Citizens were men only!

Government in Athens consisted of **a council** - chosen annually, who drew up laws and policies, then submitted them to **the assembly** - met every 10 days, had to have a quorum of 6 000, debated suggestions of council; **military commanders (strategoi)** - elected annually, reported to assembly.

Background

In democratic Greece (demos = people and kratos = rule) citizens performed certain duties. One of these was to participate in the running of the legal system. No lawyers existed and anyone accused of an offence had to conduct their own case.

Courts would have a jury of at least 200 men. This was to cut out bribery and intimidation of jurors. Any citizen wanting to serve as a juror went to the court. Usually there were too many people so a kleroteria was used to select jurors for that day. A water clock was used to limit the time allowed to each speaker in court.

When a verdict had to be reached, special tokens were issued, one for the innocent verdict and one for the guilty.

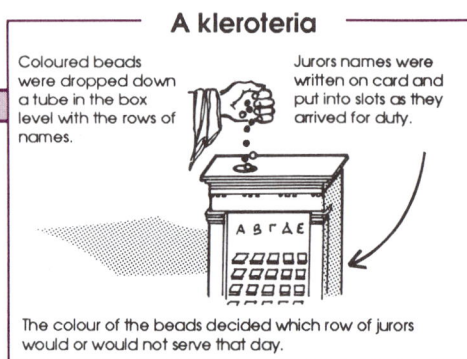

A kleroteria

Coloured beads were dropped down a tube in the box level with the rows of names.

Jurors names were written on card and put into slots as they arrived for duty.

Α Β Γ Δ Ε

The colour of the beads decided which row of jurors would or would not serve that day.

Developments

- Set up a model court-room scene and act out the sentencing of someone for a crime.
- Discuss how the Greek legal system differs from your own. - the jury, the defence, the prosecution, etc.
- Research other aspects of the Democratic system in Ancient Greece: the assembly, the council. Discuss the differences between the political system in Ancient Greece and the one existing in your own country. Which do you think is the better? Why?
- Compare the systems of government in Athens and Sparta Draw diagrams to illustrate the differences between the two systems - one could be a triangle divided into four to show hierarchy, one could be a triangle divided equally into three.
- Athens is remembered as the worlds first democracy, but women slaves and foreigners had no say in government. Talk about this.
- Compare the system of government in Ancient Greece with the system of government in this country today. Draw a matrix to show the comparison.
- Make various kinds of time mechanisms, e.g. a water clock as above, a sand timer or a candle clock.
  - What can these be best made out of?
  - How can these be tested?
  - How can the children best record their results?
- The Ancient Greeks did not believe that all men are born equal. They had many slaves. Aristotle said it was a law of nature that the free should rule over the slave. Discuss the idea of slavery, but stress that it is important for historians to judge the ancients in their own terms.

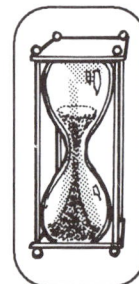

Government and the Law

Here are 3 objects used in the legal system of Ancient Greece.
Match the diagrams with their names and their use.
Talk about the differences between the legal system of Ancient Greece and the one we have today.

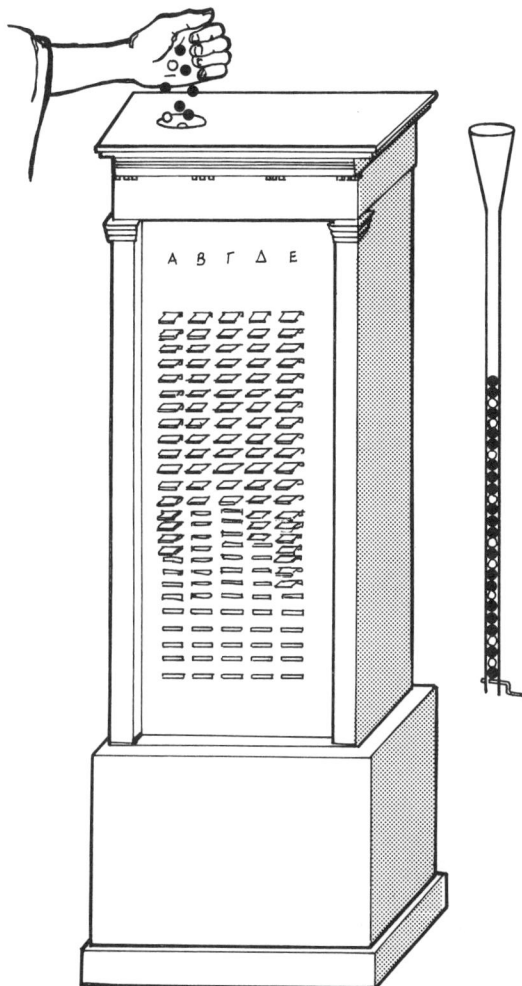

● How did they work?

Used to select the names of jurors on a daily basis.	THE KLEROTERIA
Used by jurors in court to reach a verdict.	GUILTY OR INNOCENT TOKENS
THE WATER CLOCK	Used to time speeches in the court.

Aims

A game to familiarise pupils with the symbols associated with the Greek number system.

Background

The Greek numerals

A	-1	Ξ	-60
B	-2	O	-70
r	-3	π	-80
⌒	-4	?	-90
E	-5	٩	-100
F	-6	﹥	-200
Z	-7	T	-300
I-I	-8	Υ	-400
Θ	-9	Φ	-500
I	-10	X	-600
K	-20	Ψ	-700
λ	-30	Ω	-800
M	-40	ﲀ	-900
N	-50		

● Each Greek numeral has a corresponding Greek letter. Using dictionaries and other reference sources complete a chart like the following:

Greek numerical symbol	Position in Greek alphabet	Name
A	1st letter of alphabet	Alpha
B	2nd letter of alphabet	Beta
r	3rd letter of alphabet	Gamma

Activity

● Photocopy on to card if possible. Cut out and play.
● Spread dominoes face down on table top. Each player chooses five. Dominoes remaining are moved to one side and used to draw from as the game proceeds.
● Player with the highest double domino places it on the table.
● Play moves to the left. Second player tries to match a domino to one end or side of the double. Play continues in this way, players always placing dominoes lengthwise rather than at right angles, except in the case of doubles. If a player cannot match dominoes at any time then a domino must be taken from the pile.
● Play continues until one player has used all dominoes or until no one can play. The player with no dominoes or the least number of points wins.

Developments

● Create variations of the domino game and write out the rules for others to follow.
● Try writing Greek numerals with different implements: in clay with a clay tool, with a stick or a twig and thick paint, with a broad-tipped pen.
● Use the symbols to make up simple calculations:

$$4 \quad + \quad 2 \quad = \quad 6 \qquad 8 \quad + \quad 1 \quad = \quad 9$$
$$⌒ \quad + \quad B \quad = \quad F \qquad \text{I-I} \quad + \quad A \quad = \quad Θ$$

● Use the number system and make up other simple games like 'Snap', 'Snakes and Ladders' (Columns and Steps!).
● Compare different number systems, e.g. Roman, and notice for example: similarities and differences between them; the absence of zero in some systems; the influence of one system on another.
● DUO = 2
  TREIS = 3
  PENTE = 5
  HEX = 6
  OCTO = 8
  DECO = 10
  Collect examples of words including these Greek roots.
● Pythagoras was the greatest of the Greek mathematicians. His theory of the right-angled triangle can be looked at. Measure angles of triangles to develop theories about characteristics. Move a right-angled triangle through the points of the compass, tracing each stage to show how a square is created. The pattern created by the drawing can be used in the production of tile designs.

Roman Numbers

I	= one
V	= five
X	= 10
L	= 50
C	= 100
D	= 500
M	= 1000

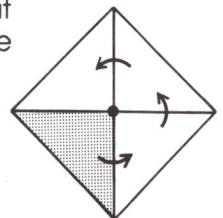

Greek Numbers

	⏢		E		F	A	A
A	B	A	r	A	⏢	A	E
A	F	B	B	B	r	B	⏢
B	E	B	F	r	r	r	⏢
r	E	r	F	⏢	⏢	⏢	E
⏢	F	E	E	E	F	F	F

Aim

Many of the words that we use today come from the Greeks. They were brought into the British Isles during the Roman occupation. This activity introduces some of these words. It requires the children to search for the meanings of the words and to become familiar with as many words of Greek origin as possible.

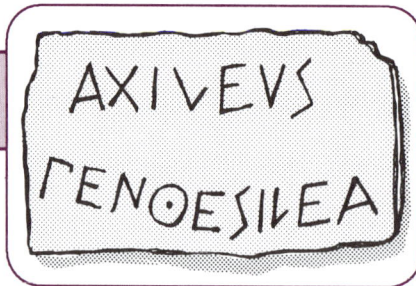

Preparation

- Make sure each group has a word temple, a word list and coloured pencil as indicated, a dictionary and paper.
- During the activity, make sure the children in each group take it in turns to go and find words.
- The time limit for this activity is the teachers decision.

The Greek Alphabet

Capital Letter	Small Letter	Capital Letter	Small Letter
A	α	N	ν
B	β	Ξ	ξ
Γ	γ	O	o
Δ	δ	Π	π
E	ε	P	ρ
Z	ζ	Σ	ς ς
H	η	T	τ
Θ	θ	Y	υ
I	ι	Φ	φ
K	k	X	χ
Λ	λ	Ψ	ψ
M	μ	Ω	ω

Activity

Instructions for the children.
- Make sure you know the meaning of all the words on your word list.
- Put each word into a sentence that makes sense.
- Colour **your words only** on the temple, with the coloured pencil as shown on your word list.
- Now look on the temple for other words you know the meaning of.
- Choose one at a time and go to another table in the class (take your temple with you).
- Say a sentence which includes the word you have chosen. If the table you have gone to has that word on their list, **they** will colour the correct block on your temple in the right colour.
  If you are incorrect in any way they will say 'Sorry, try elsewhere' or 'Sorry, wrong meaning'.
- Make sure that someone always remains at your table and that the other person looks for words.

Developments

- Using your word list, design a picture containing all your words. Write sentences or a story containing as many Greek words as possible.
- Name the groups of Greek words. Add some others to each list and then devise a worldwide version:
  - Roman (Latin)
  - Viking (Scandinavian)
  - Indian
  - Latin American (Spanish).

- Take a closer look at the structure of words. Break down the words and investigate their true meaning e.g. stethoscope. Stethos = chest; scope = to look at/ examine. Therefore the true meaning of stethoscope would be chest watcher. This activity can help in the spelling of words, but can also develop into a game. Children can take take words and attempt humorous derivations. The class has to research and find out the real derivation.

- Study the Greek alphabet and see how it is different from your own.
- Make an alphabet frieze. Each picture should be accompanied by lists of greek words. This should be displayed around the class.
- Onomatopoeic words are words in which the spelling pattern conveys the sound, e.g. crash, pop. Make a collection of such words and write sound poems. Make up new sound words for actions, e.g. what would make a floop sound?

Greek Language

RED	GREEN	YELLOW	BLUE
church priest monk bishop baptism	theatre cinema orchestra drama television	tetrahedron graph gramme ellipse statistic	ecology geology archaeology toxicology biology

PURPLE	ORANGE	BROWN	GREY
poem rhetoric onomatopoeia story monologue	megaphone telescope opisometer stethoscope telephone	physician physical pharmacy physics physiotherapy	crisis phenomenon trauma tragedy catastrophe

WORD TEMPLE

church	catastrophe	archaeology	ellipse
drama	toxicology	phenomenon	ecology
statistic	physician	tragedy	tetrahedron
biology	graph	pharmacy	baptism
trauma	poem	theatre	megaphone
physical	monologue	rhetoric	crisis
telephone	bishop	physics	geology
story	telescope	onomatopoeia	cinema
monk	orchestra	stethoscope	television
gramme	priest	physiotherapy	opisometer

This page may be photocopied for classroom use only

Aim

A legacy from Ancient Greece to the modern world is its architecture, both in terms of the remains of buildings and replicas. In this activity pupils will consider the technology of the day needed in order to construct these buildings.

Orders of architecture

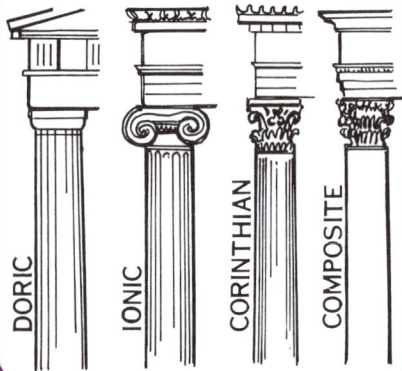

DORIC   IONIC   CORINTHIAN   COMPOSITE

Activity

The 'stones' on the pupils page provide a basic construction sequence. This can be used in different ways:
- copied and cut up so that the pupils can sequence the construction of the temple
- make a sequence of illustrations or annotated drawings for each of the statements
- groups could mime or dramatise the actions to go with each sequence of events.

Developments

- The technology within the construction can be investigated:
  - moving large objects over distances and different terrain
  - rope and pulley for lifting weights
  - joining sections with cramps, dowels and rods.
- Styles associated with Greek buildings should be investigated.
  Look at columns and the three main styles Doric, Ionic and Corinthian. What differences are there between them?
- Look at Greek words associated with buildings:
  - odeon, theatre, stadium, temple, fresco, megaron, museum, stoa, etc.
  These could be illustrated and displayed.
- Modern day examples of Greek style architecture - are there any examples near you?

Is this the only way Greeks could have moved heavy pieces of rock? How could they have transported rocks by water?

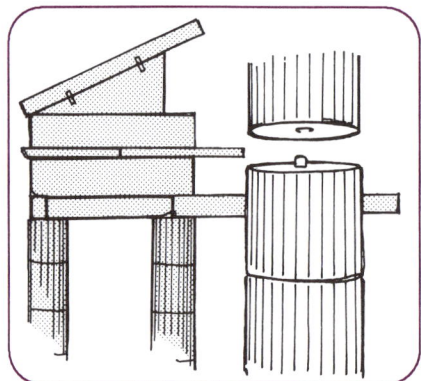

How are buildings today joined together? What has changed to make this so much easier today?

The technology within the construction can be investigated by setting the children some problems.
- The teacher builds a wall from construction materials. Groups are asked to lift an object and place in position on a base using a pulley system.
- The teacher gives each pair of children a large stone. They have to transport the stone across a set distance and a variety of landscape obstacles. This would be comparable to transporting the stone for building from the quarry to the temple building site.
- In pairs children can investigate different joints. How many different examples can be collected? How do they change according to the kinds of materials being joined? How can children best record their results?
- Using a variety of materials, children should replicate some of the joints.

Buildings

Here are the stages in building a Greek Temple. Talk about them with a friend and then put them into the correct order.

The grooves on the drums are started on the ground and finished when the column is in place.

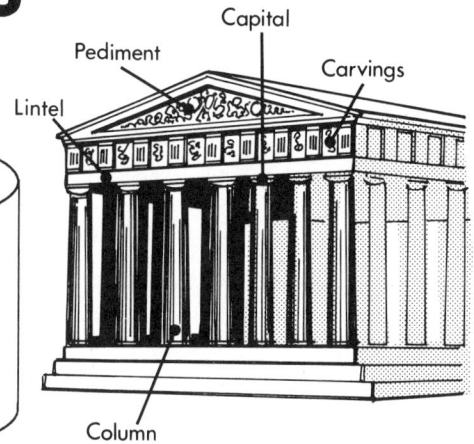

Pediment

Capital

Carvings

Lintel

Column

Blocks of stone are joined to others with metal cramps and dowels ...

A number of round pieces, called drums are put together with metal pegs to make a column ...

When in place the stones are polished.

Masons use hammers, mallets and chisels to shape the stone ...

Sculptors and artists finish the temple.

Blocks of stone are brought from the quarry on wagons ...

Levers are used to push the pieces into place ...

Ropes and pulleys are used to lift the pieces of stone ...

CONSTRUCTING A TEMPLE

This page may be photocopied for classroom use only

Objects Left Behind - Ideas Page

Aim

We know about how people in the past lived by the objects we have found that they left behind. This collaborative activity aims to help pupils discover and interpret all they can about the past through artefacts and evidence that might have been left behind.

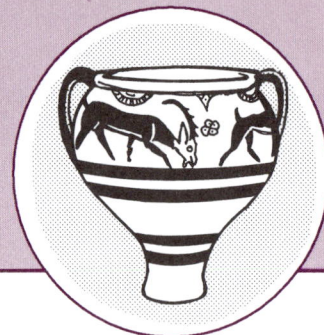

Background

Constantly, new discoveries are being made which add to our knowledge about how people lived in the past. It is like a huge jigsaw being put together and we readjust our ideas the more we get to know.

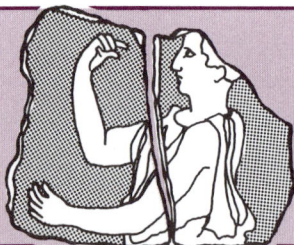

Activity

- Give each child a copy of the urn containing the six objects. Tell them that the urn and its contents were recently discovered at an archaeological site somewhere in Greece. Ask them on their own to think about who these six objects might have belonged to.
- Group the pupils together and ask them to discuss their ideas.
- Now ask each group to reach a consensus on who the owner of the items in the urn were and to share all they know about this person.
- Bring the class together and try to agree on:
  - what you know about the owner of the items
  - what can you guess about this person.

The items suggest a citizen from Athens, as citizens had to be adult male and the owl symbol was associated with Athens.

- Using the blank pot and working in pairs, the pupils should draw and write objects associated with another Greek person
  - a slave
  - a farmer
  - a soldier
  - a boy/a girl
  - a god/a goddess
  - a money changer.
- Through discussion or writing, pupils should give reasons why objects are included and associated with that person.

Developments

- Using any historical source or artefact children can ask three central historical questions:
  - What do I know?
  - What can I guess?
  - What else would I like to know?
- Pupils could exchange pots on the worksheet and discuss:
  - what is known about the owner of the items
  - what can be guessed about that person.
- Look at Greek artefacts in museums or pictures. What do these tell us about Ancient Greece?
- What would you put in a pot to tell people in the future about life today?

- Make 3D versions of the objects in the pots out of card or clay and display them. Study Greek pottery designs and make the pot itself out of clay using the coil method. Decorate when dry. It does not need to be fired.

- Look at artefacts (object or image) from any historical period. Ask each child to communicate something about that object in terms of shape, colour, size, what it is made of, if it moves or not, etc. This information can be collated to form a data base and a profile can be built up. Alternatively, the information can be used as the basis for a piece of descriptive writing or a poem.

Objects Left Behind

What do the contents of this urn tell you about its owner?

Now choose an Ancient Greek character and put objects in the pot associated with him or her.

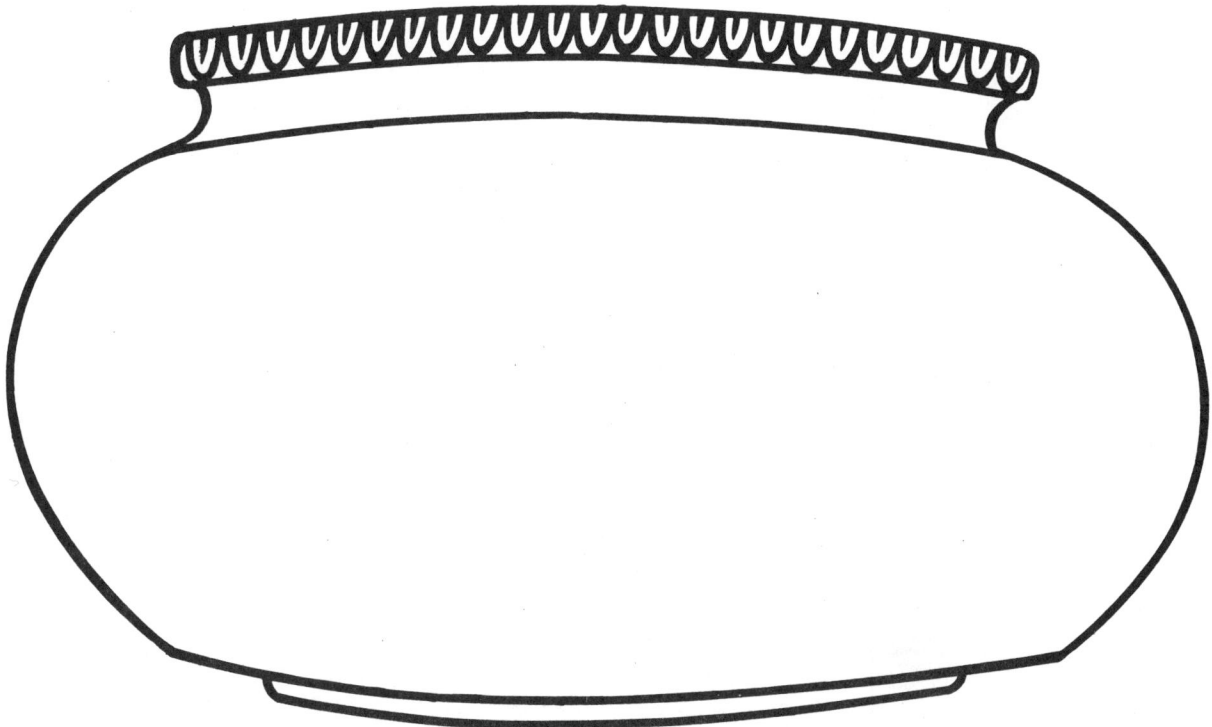

This page may be photocopied for classroom use only

Famous Greeks - Ideas Page

Aim

The purpose of this activity is to familiarise pupils with some famous people from Greek History and why they are remembered. This is demonstrated by a card game.

Background

Alexander (356-323BC) great warrior and controller of all Asia, son of **Philip of Macedon** (359-336BC). **Miltiades** (*c.*490BC) hero of Battle of Marathon. **Pythagoras** (*c.*530BC) philosopher/mathematician; discovered intervals of musical scale, theories of geometry. **Euclid** (*c.*300BC) produced first geometry book . **Archimedes** (*c.*287-212BC) mathematician scientist; calculated value of 'pi', principle of fluid displacement and made the famous screw to raise water. **Herodotus** (*c.*484-420BC) arranged historical material systematically. **Thucydides** (*c.*460-400BC) examined causes in 'Peloponnesian War'. **Xenophon** (*c.*428-354BC) biographer/historian of Sparta. **Sappho** (*c.*612BC) female lyrical poet of Lesbos. **Homer** - supposed blind author of 'The Iliad' and 'The Odyssey' - oral tradition poems probably written down in c.700BC. **Sophocles** (*c.*496-406BC) great Athenian tragic dramatist, 'Oedipus'. **Draco** (*c.*621BC) drew up harsh laws (Draconian), **Solon** (*c.*640-560BC) and **Aristides** (*c.*530-464BC) all Athenian statesmen. **Aristotle** (384-322BC), **Plato** (*c.*427-347BC) and **Socrates** (469-399BC) all great philosophers and thinkers.

Activity

On the pupils sheet are the names of some important people associated with Ancient Greece. They have been arranged into six categories and a symbol provided to aid identification.

- Photocopy the sheet on to card if possible. This game could be played like Happy Families.
- Give each group a set of cards and play the game. The winner gives the group information about a famous Greek.

Developments

- Research the background of these famous people. Create a record sheet for each set of information. This could be transferred on to the computer as a spreadsheet. Research the background of others from the period and add to the information bank.
- Write a diary for one of these people outlining details of the build up to the invention/discovery.
- Design and make a stamp commemorating the achievements of Pythagoras for example.
- As a great deal of reference work is involved in this, you could keep an on-going class matrix showing the following:

	Book Title	Page Ref.	Type of Info.
Archimedes	Osbourne	78	colour drawing and text
	Ancient Greece	85	text

This could be used as a basis for discussion on the usefulness of some books more than others.

- Create artefacts out of card or clay with the characters. Decorate and display them, e.g. a helmet for Alexander, a set of mathematical shapes for Euclid, a poem on a scroll for Homer.
- Look at other famous people throughout history. Use the same categories as in the game, or extend to other areas and look at famous people from within a special group, or from other periods of history, e.g. C S Lewis and J R R Tolkein were writers of children's stories; Pissaro, Monet and Renoir were all Impressionist artists.
- Give the children a list of questions to structure their work:
  - What is your full name?
  - When did you live?
  - Where did you live?
  - What are you remembered for?
  - What was a high/low point in your life?
- In a role play situation, characters could meet and talk.

Famous Greeks

MILITARY LEADERS	ALEXANDER THE GREAT	MILTIADES	PHILIP OF MACEDONIA

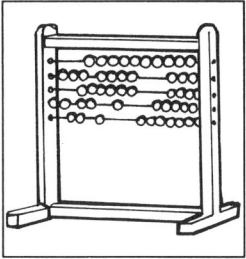

MATHEMATICIANS	PYTHAGORAS	EUCLID	ARCHIMEDES

HISTORIANS	HERODOTUS	THUCYDIDES	XENOPHON

POETS AND WRITERS	SAPPHO	HOMER	SOPHOCLES

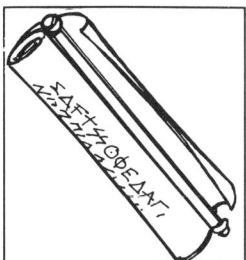

POLITICIANS	DRACO	SOLON	ARISTIDES

PHILOSOPHERS	ARISTOTLE	PLATO	SOCRATES

This page may be photocopied for classroom use only

Aim

The pupils will engage in design and art skills to produce a realistic representation of an authentic Greek object, using the themes of people and events.

Background

Draw childrens attention to the portrayal of stories and events on Greek pottery. Although Greek pottery was intended for everyday use, the Greek potters went to a great deal of effort to paint mostly scenes from everyday life on the pots.

Now, these pots give us vital clues about life in Greece at that time. Border details are also worth looking at, as are the colours used, mostly terracotta, black and white.

Activity

After looking and talking about some examples, the pupils design a plate to show a god or goddess with their associated symbols (see Who's Who on page 3 for information). Paper plates can then be used to transfer design ideas.

Developments

- Stories and events were displayed on pottery. Select a Greek story or myth and illustrate scenes on to a plate or pot.
- Draw a comparison with modern day commemorative plates and mugs. Make a collection of these alongside your home-made Greek earthenware.
- Investigate other stories on plates - The Willow Pattern story.
- Use other art media to make a design - embroidery, quilting, weaving, clay relief.
- Build up a class collection of Greek border patterns that can be used to decorate other pieces of work.
- Each child could design a plate that depicts something related to themselves, e.g. their family, where they live, an event from their life.
- The British Museum has many Ancient Greek children's toys made in clay:
  - a jointed doll
  - a whip top
  - a rattle in the form of a pig.
  Choose one of these objects and discuss how they would have been made and what problems would have occured in their manufacture:
  - how were the doll's limbs jointed?
  - how was the top made to spin?
  - what was put inside the pig to make it rattle?
  Make one of these toys and decorate it accordingly.

- Greek houses were often decorated in wall frescoes (paintings done on wet plaster). Make plaster of Paris and pour into a shoe box lid. Just before it is set, paint a Greek scene on to the surface. These make interesting wall plaques.
- Greeks were fascinated by columns and straight lines. Practise perspective drawings of rows of columns to create an illusion of receding depth.

Art and Design

Around the border of this page are some typical Greek patterns. Below you can create some of your own.

_____

_____

_____

_____

_____

_____

_____

Plan the colours you will use. Write notes to remind you how you achieved shades.

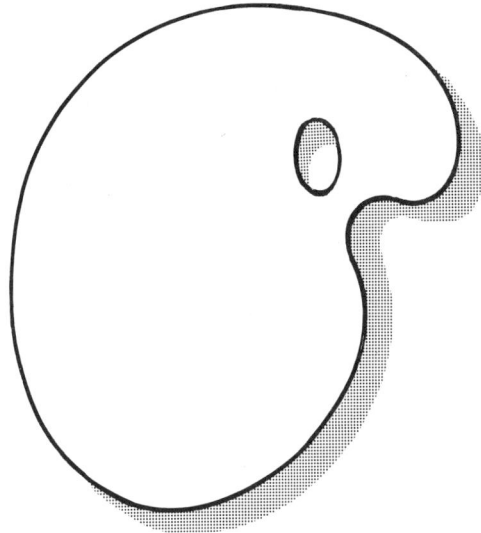

Here, you should sketch your plate design. Write notes around the outside to remind you of details you wish to include.

The Elgin Marbles - Ideas Page

Aim

This activity will explore the background of the Elgin Marbles - carvings from the Parthenon, now housed in the British Museum, through the eyes of a news reporter. Pupils will investigate the evidence surrounding the removal of the carvings from Greece and their arrival in London. They are then asked to interpret evidence.

Background

The Parthenon frieze from the Temple of Athena represents the procession for the Great Panathenaic Festival - celebrating the birthday of Athena, patron-goddess of Athens. Details show us the Gods watching the procession and many people carrying food and wine and leading sacrificial animals for the Gods. During the wars between the Greek and Turkish armies in the eighteenth century, the Turks were in control of the Parthenon. In trying to force the Turks out of the Parthenon many of the wall sculptures and artefacts in the temple were damaged. Over the next 100 years, looting of the Parthenon resulted in much being lost. Thomas Bruce (7th Lord Elgin) realised that an important part of Greek history and culture was being destroyed and arranged for the remaining sections to be shipped to London. They went on view to the public in 1816. Known as the Elgin Marbles, they remain in the British Museum to this day and are still a cause of argument as to their ownership.

Preparation

- Survey a selection of front pages from newspapers. Look at titles, headlines, layout, images.
- Discuss the fact that news arrives in newsrooms from offices around the world. The messages are telex messages and therefore contain the bare bones of stories - words are used sparingly.
- Search for information and pictures about the carvings.

Activity

- Working in pairs or threes, give each group a copy of the press releases. Altogether or one at a time - you decide.
- After the pupils have had time to talk about the press releases, as an oral activity begin to fill out the story with some details.
- Using this and any other information, the pupils have to produce a newspaper front page. Computer software could be used by some of the pupils.

Developments

- Draw up a series of questions and then interview Lord Elgin (teacher or adult in role) at a gathering of newspaper reporters.
- Design and make a poster advertising the exhibition of the Elgin Marbles at the British Museum.
- After some research create some of the carvings in clay. Make tiles first and then add on details in relief.
- The carvings showed events of importance to the Greeks. What would a set of twentieth century marbles look like?
- Who did/do the marbles really belong to? Organise a class discussion to address this issue. This could be followed by letters to the editor.

The Elgin Marbles

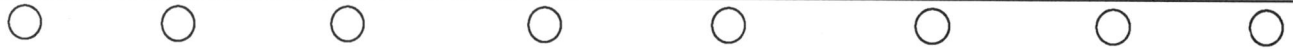

Stop Press ...
... War between Greeks and Turks continues stop Parthenon used as explosives store by Turks stop Greeks poised to attack stop

Stop Press ...   1687
... Turks under attack from Greek army stop Parthenon under threat of attack stop
... Parthenon seriously damaged stop many priceless carvings destroyed stop

Stop Press ...
... Parthenon tragedy latest stop Turks retreat stop stealing of Parthenon treasures begins stop looters take stone for own buildings stop

Stop Press ...   1803
... Lord Elgin ambassador in Greece stop will view Parthenon remains tomorrow stop
... Elgin shock at ruins stop to seek permission to bring damaged carvings home stop

Stop Press ...   1816
... Marbles to go on show stop Lord Elgin's carvings given pride of place in British Museum stop Greek officials not happy stop British public furious stop.

8 ways to help ...

There are many ideas in this book about developing and extending the photocopiable pages. Here are just eight ways to help you make the most of the **Ideas Bank** series.

1
Paste copies of the pages on to card and laminate them. The children could use water-based pens that can be wiped off, allowing the pages to be re-used.

2
Put the pages inside clear plastic wallets. They could be stored in binders for easy reference. The children's writing can again be easily wiped away.

3
If possible, save the pages for re-use. Develop a simple filing system so that the pages can be easily located for future use.

4
Use both sides of the paper. The children could write or draw on the back of the sheet, or you could photocopy another useful activity on the back.

5
Make the most of group work. Children working in small groups could use one page to discuss between them.

6
Photocopy the pages on to clear film to make overhead transparencies. The ideas can then be used time and time again.

7
Use the activity pages as ideas pages for yourself. Discuss issues and ideas with the class and ask the children to produce artwork and writing.

8
Customise the pages by adding your own activities. Supplement the ideas and apply them to your children's needs.